MW01268102

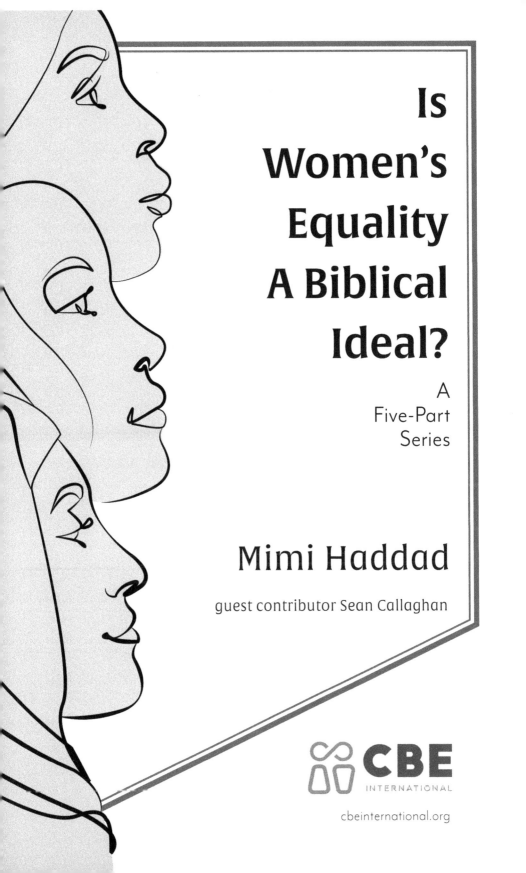

Is Women's Equality A Biblical Ideal?

A
Five-Part
Series

Mimi Haddad

guest contributor Sean Callaghan

CBE
INTERNATIONAL

cbeinternational.org

Is Women's Equality a Biblical Ideal?: A Five-Part Video Series

Published by CBE International
122 W Franklin Ave, Suite 218
Minneapolis, MN 55404
cbeinternational.org

Design: Margaret Lawrence

ISBN: 978-1-939971-94-4 (Print)
ISBN: 978-1-939971-93-7 (PDF)

Printed in the United States of America

Table Of Contents

Access Lectures Online
Visit cbe.today/ideal

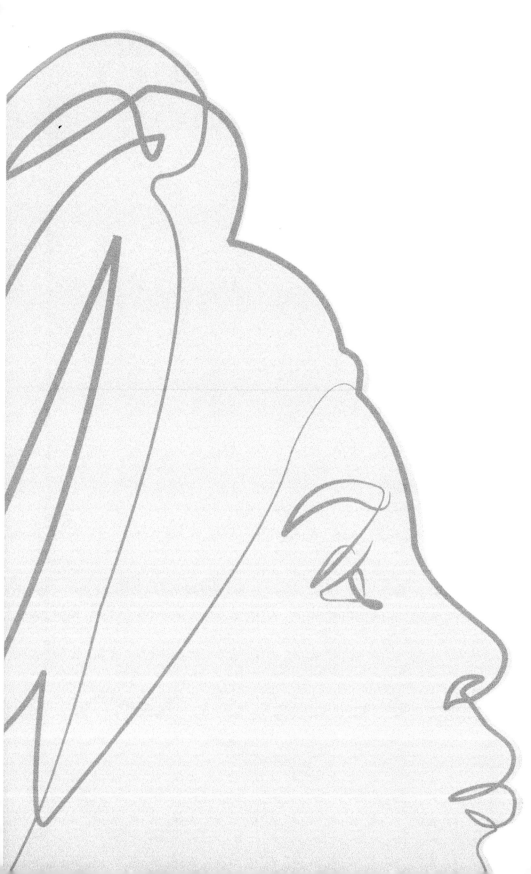

About This Book and Lecture Series

Throughout history, religion has played a significant role in shaping not only the value communities extend females, but also the opportunities for education and leadership available to women and girls. While the Christian church has opened some doors of service and leadership to women, too often Scripture has been interpreted through societal lenses that limit the roles in which women can use their God-given gifts.

Presented as a lecture series at the 2016 "Truth be Told" international conference in Johannesburg, these sessions were recorded and published under the title: *Is Gender Equality a Biblical Ideal?* This lecture series was subsequently revised for use with humanitarian and non-governmental organizations to train their leaders to effectively promote the full gifting, vocation, and authority of women—both in their organizations and the communities they work with.

Is Women's Equality a Biblical Ideal? draws on the Bible, history, and ethics to present an overview of biblical ethics and its social consequences. The series explores the biblical, historical, and social precedent for women's shared leadership in the church, the home, and the world. Topics include Old and New Testament evidence of women's leadership, the history of women's leadership in the church, and understanding power dynamics and working cross-culturally.

The lecture series and companion workbook make a wonderful resource for both personal and group study. The workbook presents an outline of the lecture content along with discussion questions for each lecture. It ends with additional resources for further study. Each of the lectures is approximately an hour long and available for free at **cbe.today/ideal**.

CBE's desire is that you find these lectures enlightening and helpful!

Lecture 1

Old Testament Considerations

Mimi Haddad

Women Challenging Patriarchy

- There is no female in Scripture who did what was right in God's eyes and who was also consistently submissive to males. This shows that what matters is not gender, but serving God and God's people.

- Women provided spiritual, moral, physical, and intellectual rescue and leadership to the people of God.

The Patriarchy Of Bible Culture

- Pater *familias.*
  - Male structuring of the ancient world.

- Women's names are rarely mentioned apart from their pater (male head).
  - Women's accomplishments were often attributed to the pater of their household.

- Semitic culture was also shaped by an honor-shame code.
  - If women in the household defied cultural practices regarding gender, this brought shame on the pater and the tribe he represented.
  - Yet Scripture honors Esther and Ruth; books in Scripture are named after them.

The Creation Of Eve

- A perfect world must include male and female.
  - Adam's aloneness is the only "not good" in a perfect world.

- Woman is created as a "strong helper," or *ezer* in Hebrew:
  - Comes from the root words "to be strong" and "to rescue."
  - Used most often to describe God's rescue of Israel.

> › Most familiar passage is Psalm 121:1–2.

The Unity Of Man And Woman

- Scripture emphasizes the unity and oneness of Adam and Eve. They share:
  - A spiritual or metaphysical substance because both are created in God's image;
  - A physical substance because Eve comes from Adam's body;
  - A common destiny because they are both given equal dominion or authority over the earth, not each other.

The Creation Account

- Genesis 1:26 (TNIV)

  Then God said, "Let us make human beings (plural) in our image (plural), in our likeness (plural), so that they may rule over the fish in the sea and the birds in the sky, over the livestock and all the wild animals, and over all the creatures that move along the ground."

- Genesis 2:24–25

  That is why a man leaves his father and mother and is united to his wife, and they become one flesh. Adam and his wife were both naked, and they felt no shame.

I lift up my eyes to the mountains— where does my help (*ezer*) come from? My help comes from the Lord, the Maker of heaven and earth.

Psalm 121:1-2

But for Adam no suitable helper (*ezer*) was found.

Genesis 2:20

The man said,
"This is now bone of my bones
and flesh of my flesh;
she shall be called 'woman,'
for she was taken out of man."

Genesis 2:23

The Garden of Eden by Lucas Cranach the Elder (1530)

So God created humankind in his own image, in the image of God he created them; male and female he created them. God blessed them and God said to them,

"Be fruitful and multiply, and fill the earth and subdue it; and have dominion over the fish in the sea and over the birds of the air and over every living thing that moves upon the earth."

Genesis 1:27–28 (NRSV)

- Genesis 3:16

  To the woman he said,

  > "I will make your pains in childbearing very severe;
  > with painful labor you will give birth to children.
  > Your desire will be for your husband,
  > and he will rule over you."

Consequences Of Sin On Gender Relations After The Fall

- Rank, authority, and hierarchy are experienced only after our covenant with God is broken.
  - Genesis 3:16 represents a tragic consequence of sin.

- Redemption will come from the woman's offspring.
  - Mary will bear Christ, who will crush evil forever.
  - Women's creational destiny as *ezer* continues after the fall.
  - Genesis 3:13–15.

The Strong Rescue Of Women Throughout The Bible And History

- Women assumed leadership as opportunities arose and through God's gifting.

- Prophets held significant positions of leadership and influence:
  - They spoke on behalf of God to the people.
  - They were leaders of leaders.
  - Female prophets provided moral, spiritual, and judicial leadership to the people of Israel.

- **Huldah**
  - Was a prophet.
  - When the book of the law was discovered, King Josiah turned to Huldah rather than to the male prophets, Zephaniah and Jeremiah.
  - 2 Kings 22:14.

- **Miriam**
  - First person Scripture calls *nabiah* ("prophet").
  - Israel refused to travel without her.
  - Numbers 12:2–16.

- **Deborah**
  - Prophet and judge.
  - Called "the mother of Israel."
  - Armies of Israel would not go into battle without her leadership.
  - Judges 4:4–5, 5:7.

- **Noadiah**
  - One of two prophets mentioned by name in Nehemiah.
  - Nehemiah 6:14.

- **Jael**
  - Honored for killing the leader of an army at war with Israel.
  - Judges 4:17–5:24.

- **Sarah**
  - "Sarai" means chief or chiefess.
  - Lived in Pharaoh's court independent of Abraham.
  - Was an independent leader of the tribe of Israel.
  - Genesis 17:15–21:12.

- **Rebekah and Rachel**
  - Rebekah orchestrates an inheritance for Jacob, the younger son, and not Esau.

- Rachel makes key decisions by giving Bilhah and Leah to her husband Jacob.
- Genesis 27:5–42; 30:1–7.

- **Tamar**
  - Continues the bloodline by deceiving her pater, Judah.
  - Judah admits she is "more righteous."
  - Genesis 38:6–26.

- **Zipporah**
  - Wife of Moses.
  - Circumcised their son.
  - She performed what later became a priestly function, performed exclusively by male priests.
  - Exodus 4:24–26.

- **Mahlah, Noah, Hoglah, Milcah, and Tirzah**
  - Five sisters who challenged male-only inheritance laws.
  - Moses gave them the right to inherit property.
  - Numbers 27:1–11.

- **Shiphrah and Puah**
  - Midwives who disobey the king by saving the lives of Hebrew babies.
  - Exodus 1:8–22.

- **Rahab**
  - Sent Israel's spies to safety.
  - She remains in control by negotiating the safety of her family.
  - She is included in the courageous and faithful in Hebrews 11:31.
  - Joshua 2.

Conclusion

- These women of courage, along with many others, are *ezers*, strong help and rescue. They served God over all human authority and in doing so fulfilled the purposes for which God created them.

- Looking at these women, it is evident that God honors leadership and authority based on courage and initiative, not based on gender.

Discussion Questions

1. Did anything surprise you about this interpretation of the text? If so, what?

2. Who was more responsible for sin, Adam or Eve, and why?

3. Do Adam and Eve suffer the consequences of sin equally?

4. If Old Testament women were praised for their leadership, even when men followed their lead (Deborah, Sarah, Rebekah, Huldah, etc.), what does this teach us about God's intentions for men and women?

5. How did these women challenge patriarchy in their day and how do they help us with the same issues today?

Lecture 2

New Testament Considerations

Mimi Haddad

Then, leaving her water jar, the woman went back to the town and said to the people, "Come, see a man who told me everything I ever did. Could this be the Messiah?" They came out of the town and made their way toward him.

John 4:28–30

4th century depiction of Jesus and the woman at the well

What Jesus Accomplished For Women

Jesus

- Spoke directly with women and allowed them to sit at his feet.

- Engaged women theologically.

- Broke social and religious restrictions related to gender.

- Demontrated value resides not in her adherence to gender roles but in her response to God's revelation in her life.

The Woman At The Well Of Sychar (John 4:7–42)

- Jesus discloses his messianic mission first to a woman and a Samaritan.

- The disciples are surprised and disappointed that Jesus talks with a woman in broad daylight.

- She becomes the first evangelist and many Samaritans come to faith through her testimony.

Women In Christ's Anointing And Resurrection

- The disciples disapprove of the woman who pours perfumed oil on Jesus.
  - Jesus corrects the disciples.

Jesus' Anointing by Alexander Rida (1874)

- She anointed the King of Glory for his work on the cross.
  - The greatest priestly anointing in history was the task of a woman.

- Christ also appeared to women after his death and burial (John 20:1–18).
  - Mary Magdalene is considered the "apostle to the apostles."

What Paul Accomplished For Women

"Nor Is There Male And Female"

- **Galatians 3:28 was**
  - Acknowledged in Christian baptism and open to all people;
  - Celebrated in the sharing of the bread and the cup;
  - Lived out each day in the Spirit in mutual deference to one another (Eph. 5:21);
  - The basis for Paul working beside slaves, Gentiles, and women in his efforts to build the church.

> When she poured this perfume on my body, she did it to prepare me for burial. Truly I tell you, wherever this gospel is preached throughout the world, what she has done will also be told, in memory of her.
>
> Matthew 26:12-13

> There is neither Jew nor Gentile, neither slave nor free, nor is there male and female, for you are all one in Christ Jesus.
>
> Galatians 3:28

> Submit to one another out of reverence for Christ.
> Wives, submit yourselves to your own husbands as
> you do to the Lord.
>
> Ephesians 5:21–22

Ephesians 5:21–22

- Paul asks Christians to submit to one another, and wives to submit to their husbands.

- Paul then asks husbands to love wives as they love their own bodies.

- Paul reframes gender and authority by placing the burden of love and service on those with power: free men.

Paul And His Female Coworkers

- Junia (Rom. 16:7)

- Phoebe (Rom. 16:1)
    - Church leader and deacon

- Priscilla (Acts 18:2–3, 18, 26; Rom. 16:3–4; 2 Tim. 4:19)
    - Is mentioned ahead of her husband in four of the six references to her;
    - Teaches Apollos in her house church;
    - May have authored Hebrews.

- Lydia, Nympha, Chloe, Apphia (Acts 16:14; Col. 4:15; 1 Cor. 1:11; Phm. 1:2)

Icons depicting Lydia (left), Priscilla and Acquila (center), and Andronicus, Athanasius, and Juna (right). Image of Lydia courtesy of eikonografos.com, used with permission.

Leadership And Spiritual Gifts

- Leadership looks radically different in the kingdom of God.

- Those who wish to be leaders must be servants.

- Paul highlights the responsibility of those who have been gifted in certain ways.

- Gifts are not given along ethnic or gender lines.

1 Timothy 2:11–12

- Paul does prohibit a group of women from teaching but not because of their gender.

- Paul uses the Greek word *authentein* rather than *exousia* for the word "authority."

- *Authentein* denotes domineering or usurped authority.

- Paul asks women to learn in silence so that when they do teach, they will teach truth.

I do not permit a woman to teach or to assume authority

over a man; she must be quiet.

1 Timothy 2:12

Historical Translations Of 1 Timothy 2:12[1]

- **The Vulgate Bible** (4th–5th century AD):"I permit not a woman to teach, neither to domineer over a man."

- **The Geneva Bible** (1560 edition): "I permit not a woman to teach, neither to usurp authority over the man."

- **King James Version** (1611):"I suffer not a woman to teach, nor usurp authority over a man."

- **The New English Bible** (1961):"I do not permit a woman to be a teacher, nor must woman domineer over man."

Qualifications For Leaders And The Gifts Of The Spirit

Elders & Overseers: 1 Timothy 3:2–3	Deacons: 1 Timothy 3:8	Widows: 1 Timothy 3:11	Fruit of the Spirit Galatians 5:22–26
Temperate, sensible, respectable, hospitable, an apt teacher, not a drunkard, not violent but gentle, not quarrelsome, and not a lover of money…	Serious, not double-tongued, not indulging in much wine, not greedy for money…	Women likewise must be serious, not slanderers, but temperate, faithful in all things…	Love, joy, peace, patience, kindness, generosity, faithfulness, gentleness, and self-control…

Discussion Questions

1. What is most surprising or inspiring about Jesus' interactions with women?

2. What is most surprising or inspiring about Paul's teachings or interactions with women?

3. What passages do you find most challenging regarding gender and authority?

4. How does reading these passages within their historical context inform your interpretation?

5. How do the examples of the women in the New Testament challenge your view of women leaders today?

Lecture 3

A Historical Perspective

Mimi Haddad

- **The Patriarchal View**
  - Men and women are both created by God, but women are (in their being and nature) inferior to men. Therefore women are to submit to men.
  - Unequal in being: Unequal in authority

- **The Egalitarian View**
  - Men and women are both equally:
    - › Created in God's image.
    - › Given dominion in Eden.
    - › Responsible for and distorted by sin.
    - › Redeemed by Christ and gifted by the Holy Spirit.
    - › Responsible for using their gifts in service to Christ.
  - Equal in being: Equal in authority

- **The Complementarian View**
  - Men and women are created in God's image as equals, but women have different "roles" or "functions" than men. Women's "role" or "function" means that women are to submit to male authority.
  - Equal in being: Unequal in authority

Ontology

- Derived from the Greek *ontos* meaning "of being" and *logos* meaning "the study of," ontology is the philosophical study of the being. It is a branch of philosophy known as metaphysics.

- Ontology is the study of being, nature, or essence, assessed through comparisons. To assume the ontological inferiority of any group is to assert that their being, nature, or essence is less moral, rational, or strong compared to another group's being, nature, or essence.

The Influence Of Greek Philosophy

- **Aristotle** (384–322 BC): "It is the best for all tame animals to be ruled by human beings. For this is how they are kept alive. In the same way, the relationship between the male and the female is by nature such that the male is higher, the female lower, the male rules and the female is ruled."[1]

- **Plato** (427–347 BC): "It is only males who are created directly by the gods and are given souls. Those who live rightly return to the stars, but those who are 'cowards or [lead unrighteous lives] may with reason be supposed to have changed into the nature of women'… obviously it is only men who are complete human beings and can hope for ultimate fulfillment; the best a woman can hope for is to become a man."[2]

The Patriarchy Of Greek And Roman Cultures

- Vast numbers of baby girls were left to die after birth.

- Women rarely participated in philosophy or politics.

- Women rarely joined meals or social gatherings with males.

- Males had many sexual partners including slaves, female prostitutes, and boys/men, in addition to their wives.

- Marriage was to ensure legitimate heirs.

The Shared Authority Of Early Christians

- Christians rescued abandoned baby girls.

- Women participated in the agape meals.

- Women served in many positions of leadership.

- Christian women were martyred beside males for their influence.

- Christian marriages were monogamous.

- Paul tells husbands to love their wives, and sacrifice themselves for them. Wives and husbands share equal authority.

Paul's Transformation

- **Menahoth 43b–44a**
  - "Thank you [God] for not making me a Gentile, a woman or a slave."

- **Galatians 3:28**
  - There is neither Jew nor Gentile, neither slave nor free, nor is there male and female, for you are all one in Christ Jesus.

The Church Fathers

- **Irenaeus** (130–202 AD): "Both nature and the law place the woman in a subordinate condition to the man."[3]

- **Augustine** (354–430 AD): "Nor can it be doubted, that it is more consonant with the order of nature that men should bear rule over women, than women over men."[4]

- **Chrysostom** (347–407 AD): "The woman taught once, and ruined all. On this account therefore he saith, let her not teach…for the sex is weak and fickle…"[5]

John Polkinghorne's Bottom-Up Thinking

- Polkinghorne's bottom-up thinking suggests that a critical analysis of any field will always require a healthy skepticism of the assumptions made by previous scholarly traditions. Polkinghorne calls this "bottom-up thinking." That is, one must allow the facts to stand on their own, even if in doing so we confront some deeply held assumptions.

Paula (347–404 AD)

- Jerome wrote: "There are people, O Paula and Eustochium [Paula's daughter,] who take offense at seeing your names at the beginning of my works. These people do not know that Huldah prophesied when men were mute; while Barak trembled, Deborah saved Israel; that Judith and Esther delivered from supreme peril the children of God…Is it not to women that our Lord appeared after his resurrection? Yes, and the men could then blush for not having sought what women had found."[6]

Macrina (324–379 AD)

- Sister to Basil the Great and Gregory of Nyssa, both church fathers.

- Basil, famous for his defense of the Nicene Creed, and Gregory, known for his theological development of the Holy Spirit, both credit their older sister for their theological education. Macrina's holy life attracted many followers, and as her fame spread she became known simply as "the teacher."

Apollonia

- Deacon in the Church of Alexandria

- Martyred in 249 AD

Apollonia's Ordination Prayer
For Women Deacons

O Eternal God, the Father of our Lord Jesus Christ, the
Creator of man and of woman, who did replenish with your
Spirit Miriam, and Deborah, and Anna, and Huldah; who
did not disdain that your only begotten Son should be born
of a woman; who also in the tabernacle of the testimony, and
in the temple, did ordain women to be keepers of your holy
gates,—do now also look down upon this servant, who is
to be ordained to the office of a deacon, and grant her your
Holy Spirit to "cleanse her from all filthiness of flesh and
spirit," that she may worthily discharge the work which is
committed to her to your glory. Amen.[7]

The Middle Ages And Women's Leadership

- **Aquinas:** "[T]he image of God is in man and also in woman...In relation to something secondary, it is true that the image of God is in man in a way not found in woman. For man is origin and goal of woman, just as God is origin and goal of the whole creation."[8]

The Middle Ages

Teresa of Avila	Catherine of Siena	Hildegard von Bingen
1515–1582	1347–1380	1098–1179

John Calvin (1509–1564)

- "Women are not to *assume authority over the man*; for the very reason, why they are forbidden to teach, is, that it is not permitted by their *condition*. They are subject, and to teach implies the rank of power or authority" (emphasis added).[9]

John Knox (1513–1573)

- "Nature, I say, does paint [women] forth to be weak, frail, impatient, feeble, and foolish; and experience has declared them to be inconstant, variable, cruel... Since flesh is subordinate to spirit, a woman's place is beneath man's."[10]

The Reformation

Jeanne D'Albret
1528—1572

Anne Askew
1521—1546

Lady Jane Grey
1537—1554

Catherine Parr
1512—1548

Early Methodist And Holiness Movement

Susanna Wesley
1669—1742

Phoebe Palmer
1807—1874

Phoebe Palmer

- "I have not a slight apprehension that God has called me to stand before the people, and proclaim His truth…and so truly has He set His seal upon it…in the conversion of thousands of precious souls, the sanctification of a multitude of believers, that even Satan does not seem to question that my call is divine."[11]

A.J. Gordon (1836–1895)

- In the New Covenant, those who had once been viewed as inferior by natural birth attain a new spiritual status through the power of the Holy Spirit. For God's gifting no longer rests on a "favored few, but upon the many, without regard to race, or age, or sex."[12]

Katharine Bushnell (1855–1946)

- "Just so long as men imagine that a system of caste is taught in the Word of God, and that they belong to the upper caste while women are of the lower caste; and just so long as they believe that mere flesh—fate—determines the caste to which one belongs; and just so long as [men] believe that… Genesis 3:16 [teaches] 'your desire shall be for your husband, and he shall rule over you'…the destruction of young women into a prostitute class [will] continue."[13]

Bushnell's Survey Of Genesis[14]

- Adam and Eve were both created in the image of God.

- Adam and Eve were both equally called to be fruitful and to exercise dominion in Eden.

- Eve was not the source of sin, and God does not curse women because of Eve.

- It was Satan, not God, who inspired the domination of men over women.

- God bestows leadership on those who do what is right in God's sight, regardless of their gender, birth order, nationality, or class.

Bushnell On Paul

- In assessing Paul, Bushnell determined that the apostle affirmed the authority and leadership of women provided their leadership was neither domineering nor abusive (1 Tim. 2:12); that those who teach must understand and advance the truth concerning the gospel (1 Tim. 2:11–12, Acts 18:26, Rom. 16:1–5, 7, 12–13, 15), and that when women pray and prophesy in public they are not disruptive, either by their clothing or through their chatter (1 Cor. 11:5, 14:34). Ultimately, Bushnell insists that women's status is found not in the fall, but in Christ's completed work on Calvary.[15]

Jessie Penn-Lewis (1861–1927)

- "The 'old creation,' in its form of 'Jew and Gentile,' must die to make way for a new creation 'after the image of Him' that created him; where... there can be neither Jew nor Greek, there can be neither bond nor free, there can be no male and female; for ye are one in Christ Jesus. In the face of these words we cannot wonder that the Cross is a stumbling-block, and its message likened to a sword or knife, for it cuts deep into the very core of the pride of the old creation. God's cure...is not a superficial one...Nothing but the Cross will bring about the unity He desires."[16]

Does Scripture Teach Male Authority?

- All Christians should submit to one another (Eph. 5:21).

- Wives have authority over their husband's body and husbands have authority over their wife's body (1 Cor. 7:4).

- Junia was outstanding among the apostles (Rom. 16:7).

- Female prophets declare the truth of God (1 Cor. 11:3–5, 14:31, Acts 2:17, 21:9, Luke 2:36–38).

- Women were deacons (Rom. 16:1–3).

- Women were house church leaders (Acts 16:14–15; Rom. 16:13–15; 1 Cor. 1:11, 16:19; Philem. 1:2; 2 John 1:1).

- Women were teachers (Acts 18:26).

- Women were evangelists (Rom. 16:3, Phil. 4:3, Philem. 1:2).

- Women and slaves do the heavy lifting of the gospel (Rom. 16:7, 1 Cor. 16:15–16).

Discussion Questions

1. Have you heard the argument that women and men are equal in being but unequal in authority? Do you agree with this statement? Why or why not?

2. Who are your favorite women in history and why?

3. Why do you think Christians rarely hear about women leaders in the church?

4. What can be done to make the history of women better known?

5. How do we recover their histories?

Lecture 4

Opposing the Curse: Dismantling Patriarchy

Mimi Haddad

Ideas Have Consequences

Ancient Greece

Ideas and Teachings

- Aristotle: "…the male is higher, the female is lower, the male rules, the female is ruled."[1]

Consequences

- Female babies were abandoned at birth.

- Patriarchy excluded females from
    - Social gatherings of males;
    - Political and philosophical determination;
    - Control over children, property, and self.

- Marriages were not monogamous.

Brahmanism (In Many Communities)

Ideas and Teachings

- Females are believed to possess a temper or nature that is mutable [or inconstant].

- "Females are said to be destitute of strength and also of knowledge. They are viewed as impure as falsehood itself [and] that is a fixed rule."[2]

Consquences

- Females do not recite sacred texts in public.

- Females are expected to submit to male authority throughout life; to their fathers, husbands, sons, and grandsons.

- The gods are rarely praised for the birth of girls.

- Ultrasound is used to select for gender.

- Though illegal, girls remain sex-slaves in Hindu temples. They are called *deva dasi*, or the "Devil's whore."

Islam (In Many Communities)

Ideas and Teachings

- "The character of women is like a crooked rib, a crookedness that is inherent and incurable."[3]

- Men have authority over women because God made the one superior to the other.

Consequences

- Females are expected to submit to male authority throughout their lives.

- Honor killings occur when females are believed to be promiscuous.

- Genital cuttings are performed to preserve marital fidelity.

- Females are not relied on as witnesses in court.

- Medical treatment for females is only provided when female health care professionals are available.
  - Women are frequently excluded from public education and from work outside the home.

Nazi Germany

Ideas and Teachings

- Nazi re-education of Germany triumphantly declared: "[T]here are only a few people left in Germany who are not clear about the fact that the Jew is not, as previously thought, distinct from 'Christians'… only in that [they are] of another religion, and is therefore a German like all of the rest of us, but rather that [they belong] to a different race than we do. The Jew belongs to a different *race*; that is what is decisive" (emphasis added).[4]

Consequence

- Six million Jews died in Nazi concentration camps during World War II.

Slavery In America

Ideas and Teachings

- "The African race is constitutionally inferior to the white race."[5]

- "Slavery, in the United States, is founded on color, it is…[based on the belief in the] native and indestructible inferiority…[of] race."[6]

Consequences

- Slavery mocked biblical morality in manifold ways. Marriages were ignored, girls and women were defiled, and murders and maimings were common.

- The Emancipation Proclamation did little to eliminate ethnic abuse, because the root idea—ethnic inferiority—was not addressed. Therefore, freed by legal decree, African Americans quickly encountered Jim Crow laws.

Christianity

Ideas and Teachings

- **Chrysostom:** (347–407) "The woman taught once, and ruined all. On this account therefore he saith, let her not teach…*for the sex is weak and fickle…*" (emphasis added).[7]

- **Augustine:** (354–430) "Nor can it be doubted, that it is more consonant with the order of *nature* that men should bear rule over women, than women over men" (emphasis added).[8]

- **John Knox:** (1514–1572) *Nature,* I say, does paint [women] forth to be weak, frail, impatient, feeble, and foolish; and experience has declared them to be inconstant, variable, cruel…a woman's place is beneath man's" (emphasis added).[9]

- **John Calvin:** (1509–1564) Woman should not hold "authority over the man; for the very reason, why they are forbidden to teach, is, that it is not permitted by their *condition*" (emphasis added).[10]

Consequence

Mark Driscoll (1970–) "[W]hen it comes to leading in the church, women are unfit because they are more gullible and easier to deceive than men....[W]omen who fail to trust [Paul's] instruction...are much like their mother Eve...Before you get all emotional like a woman in hearing this, please consider the content of the women's magazines at your local grocery store that encourages liberated women in our day to watch porn with their boyfriends...and master oral sex [with] men who have no intention of marrying them...and ask yourself if it doesn't look like the Serpent is still trolling the garden and that the daughters of Eve aren't gullible in pronouncing progress, liberation, and equality."[11]

Challenging Religious Ideals That Devalue

Catherine Booth
1829—1890

Co-founder of
the Salvation
Army in
1865 with
her husband
William.

Josephine Butler
1828—1906

Founder of the
International
Abolitionist
Federation
to oppose
government-
supported
prostitution
abroad.

Dr. Katharine
Bushnell, MD
1855—1946

Head of the
Social Purity
Department of
the Women's
Christian
Temperance
Union
(WCTU)

Bushnell On British Brothels In India

"We walked through the lines of encampments…[and] went on to the little tents for women…and took their testimony…hearts melted and tears flowed, and they were eager to tell us how they had been brought against their will, or by trickery or thoughtlessly, into such a horrible life. More than once…they would not let us [go] till they prayed…to help them to get out of virtual imprisonment. We interviewed about 500 such pitiful creatures."[12]

"How can officials of high standing as Christian gentlemen be so indifferent to the wrongs of women and girls, so complacent in dealing with the sensuality of men, and so ready to condone their offences against decency…[men who sent orders] to under-officials to secure 'younger and more attractive girls' for the British soldiers…

Sir John Bowring, who wrote those beautiful hymns like 'Watchman, Tell Us of the Night' and 'In the Cross of Christ I Glory' by his legislation at Hong Kong brought into existence ordinances making it punishable for any Chinese girl to live but with her owner, who kept her for immoral purposes…acts which cannot but seep hundreds, perhaps thousands, of girls into prostitution."[13]

Beliefs Shape World View

A Patriarchal Worldview

- **Epistemology or knowledge:** God has revealed in Scripture that males are superior to females in their being.

- **Ontology or being:** Males, in their being, are superior to females.

- **Teleology or purpose:** Males' destiny is to hold authority, females' is to submit. This is best for all marriages, families, churches, and communities.

- **Ethics or justice:** Unilateral male authority advances God's justice (this view has been noted as the cause of unhappiness and abuse in families and communities).[14]

An Egalitarian Worldview

- **Epistemology or knowledge:** God has revealed in Scripture that males and females are created and gifted equally.

- **Ontology or being:** Men and women are equal in being.

- **Teleology or purpose:** Biology is not destiny. Rather, God calls and gifts all Christians for service and leadership based on their character, intimacy with Christ, and their God-given gifts.

- **Ethics or justice:** The dignity and equality of males and females extends to positions of leadership and authority in church, home, and society. Superiority, patriarchy, dominance, and abuse based on gender is challenged.

Findings of Christian Humanitarians Today[15]

Cambodia

Ideas and Teachings

- Men are as pure gold, women are white cloth.

Consequences

- Women rarely work outside the home. When females leave the sex industry they often feel unwelcome and are marginalized in evangelical churches. Evangelical churches in Cambodia tend to support male-only models of leadership. The question is, do male-only models of leadership reinforce the inferiority of females?

Kenya And Uganda

Ideas and Teachings

- Since Adam was created first, Genesis is interpreted as showing male preference.

- The word "head" in Scripture is understood to mean authority instead of source.

- Creation myths in African religions underline the superiority of men.

Consequences

- Boys receive priority in education and nutrition.

- Female genital mutilation (FGM) is widely practiced because females are viewed as innately promiscuous.

- Women are often barred from owning property, even in areas where the law specifically allows them to.

- There is no term for "domestic violence" in African culture. Rather, men are said to "discipline" females, which means to exert violence over them because women need male "discipline."

- Christian missionary organizations often follow male-only models of leadership.

China

Ideas and Teachings

- **Christianity:** Women are seen as helpers, inferior, and weaker vessels.

- **Buddhism:** A woman can never become Buddha unless she is reincarnated as a man. Many Chinese characters associate bad luck and evil with the female gender, and these words are still used.

- After the Qing Dynasty, leaders sought ways to release the gifts of women because women comprise half the population.

Consequences

- Under the one-child policy, parents and mothers often aborted girl babies.

- In churches, abuse and sexual harassment are not taken seriously.

- Even when women start Christian organizations, men take the credit for it in their autobiographies.

- Leadership in Chinese churches, especially in the US, is based on gender.

India

Ideas and Teachings

- "There is nothing else that is more sinful than women."[16]

- "Animals, illiterates, lower castes, and women should be subject to beating."[17]

- "She waits on her husband as a god, and surrenders her own will completely to his."[18]

Consequences

- Most churches do not approve of egalitarian marriage and all oppose divorce, even in the case of abuse.

- Women are told they are impure during menstruation. Their voices are not to be heard in public.

- Childlessness is blamed on women.

- Widows are assumed to bring bad luck.

- Divorce is believed to be the woman's fault.

- There are few Christian organizations in India headed by a woman.

An Observation

"It seemed that no matter how I tried to slice it, spin it, or soften it; at the end of the day, however much the gap was minimized… By making the husband the default tie-breaker within the home, even in the best of marriages, there is still the subtle message that the wisdom of a woman is less than that of a man. By making the position of leadership within spiritual community inaccessible based solely on gender, a glass ceiling is imposed that speaks volumes to the souls of women and where they stand in social order, even perhaps before God…Ideas do have consequences, and…holding this theological position became a problem of injustice for me.

Years ago my vocation began taking me to various parts of the globe dealing with issues of injustice. Time and again I encountered cultural practices that subjugated and subverted women, most always justified through long standing traditional or religious values and mores. Whether through a process or an abrupt change, it was not until those values were challenged and replaced that breakthroughs for women were realized. I began challenging my own beliefs."[19]

—Lance Robinson
Founder and president of *Equitas*

Discussion Questions

1. What are the cultural messages (subtle or not so subtle) that devalue females where you work?

2. How have religious examples or teachings devalued females in your context?

3. How have you or others challenged a cultural or religious devaluation of females?

4. What are positive examples, culturally or religiously, that extend equal value to females?

5. What are effective ways, from your experience, to represent females' value equally relative to males'?

Working Cross-Culturally

Sean Callaghan

The Battle For Gender Equality Is Ultimately A Power Struggle

- Gender-based violence is more about power than about arousal.

- Patriarchy is more about power than about protection.

Power Dynamics

- Power dynamics differ depending on cultural values.

- Geert Hofstede's work on culture mapping can help us understand these differences.[1]

- Two of Hofstede's indicators that are relevant are power distance and individualism.

Power Distance

- The extent to which the less powerful people in a society accept that power is distributed unequally.

- High power distance: Individuals readily accept their place in the hierarchy and find it impossible to challenge those in power.

- Low power distance: Individuals readily challenge those in power because they simply don't accept the power distance in the first place.

- The Global North generally has a low power distance. The Global South tends to exhibit high power distance.

- In the realm of education, areas with low power distance value critical thinking and students are encouraged to challenge existing ideas that are presented by the teacher.

- High power distance areas value experts. High grades are given to students who can best remember and recite what the teacher has taught.

- It's important to consider power distance as we develop programs for other cultural contexts.

Individualism And Collectivism

- In individualistic societies, the focus is on the individual.

- In collectivistic societies, the focus is on a group of some kind, like a clan, a family, or a tribe.

- People in individualistic societies form their identity based on how they can stand out from the group.

- People in collectivistic societies find their meaning in the crowd, in being part of the group.

- In individualistic societies, children are often brought up by nuclear families or single parents, while in collectivistic societies, an entire village helps raise a child.

- Individualistic societies tend to have criminal justice systems that focus on punishment, while collectivistic societies tend to have more restorative approaches.

Comparison Of Two Contexts: The US And East Africa

- Both are very Christian contexts, both have a strong history of patriarchy, both have a theology of patriarchy in the church.

- Based on this, presumably, material and programming would be interchangable between the US and East Africa. There are, however, key differences that Hofstede illuminates.

- As the figure below shows, the United States and East Africa are very different when it comes to both individualism and collectivism and power distance.

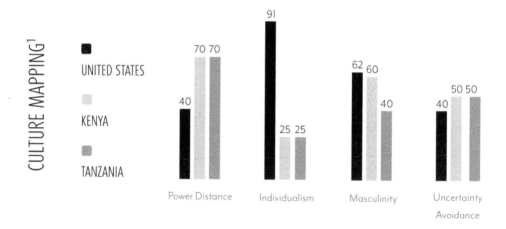

CULTURE MAPPING[1]

UNITED STATES

KENYA

TANZANIA

| | Power Distance | Individualism | Masculinity | Uncertainty Avoidance |

Power Distance: 40, 70, 70
Individualism: 91, 25, 25
Masculinity: 62, 60, 40
Uncertainty Avoidance: 40, 50, 50

Other Cultural Differences To Consider

- The urban/rural divide
  - Rural communities are more conservative than urban ones and urban communities have greater access to global media.
  - Media help give a more nuanced picture of gender relations but also influences gender stereotyping.

- The Christian nature of our work
  - Christian faith is often used to reinforce stereotypes about women.
  - Urban areas have greater access to television which means access to conservative Christian programs from the US. These often help reinforce patriarchal theology.

The Impact Of Choice

- Many in the Global North are used to a multitude of choices, while those in the Global South have very few.

- Many programs encourage people to simply change the way they think or act, but don't take into account that choice may not be a luxury that individuals have in their culture. This is especially true in gender-related issues.

- The level at which change takes place is often one of the most important factors in spreading important ideas. In the Global North, change is catalyzed at the individual level. In the Global South, working with individuals is often not effective because of the collectivism and high power distance that is prevelant in these cultures. Often the most effective place to bring about change in these cultures is at middle management.

Programming Implications

- In the Global North, a Bible study might be an effective tool. In the Global South, training pastors and bishops might be the most effective approach.

- A campaign against gender-based violence that calls men individually might work well in the Global North while meeting with community leaders to develop a campaign for the entire community would be more effective in the Global South.

- While the effects on programming are different, the underlying theology between both approaches is the same.

Implications On Organizational Partnerships

- Those in the Global North often come to a partnership with power and influence, which makes it difficult for those from a culture with a high power distance to challenge them. This can create frustrations that stem from the miscommunication.

- Four possible states in a partnership are detailed in the graphic below. Ideally, the partnership moves in the direction of the arrow.

- Ultimately it's up to those in power to create a space for collaboration in a way that complements the culture of the partner with less power.

- Taking all of these cultural factors into account can create an enviroment where empowerment and empathy create true and lasting change for gender equality.

Power Dynamics

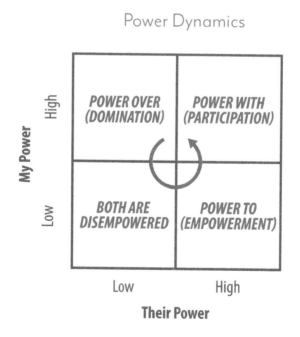

Discussion Questions

1. Where do you see power distance and individualism exhibited in the cultures of the Global North? Can you think of any effects these have had on gender norms in these societies?

2. Have you ever had trouble communicating with someone from another culture or subculture? What differences made the process difficult?

3. How has the luxury of choice played a role in your journey to gender equality?

4. Brainstorm a few strategies for influencing gender equality in the context of the Global North. Then, given what you know about cultural differences, consider how you would adapt these to be effective in the Global South. What weaknesses do you see?

5. Imagine that you represent an organization from the Global South that is partnering with one from the Global North. How would you feel if your partners from the Global North failed to take the high power distance of your culture into account?

Credits

Dr. Mimi Haddad Author

Dr. Mimi Haddad is president of CBE International. She is a graduate of Gordon-Conwell Theological Seminary and holds a PhD in historical theology from the University of Durham, England. Palmer Theological Seminary of Eastern University awarded Mimi an Honorary Doctorate of Divinity in 2013. Haddad is part of the leadership of Evangelicals for Justice and is a consultant for World Vision. She has written more than one hundred articles and blog posts and has contributed to ten books. She is also an editor and a contributing author of *Global Voices on Biblical Equality: Women and Men Serving Together in the Church*. Mimi is an adjunct assistant professor at Fuller Theological Seminary (Houston, TX). She and her husband, Dale, live in the Twin Cities, MN.

Sean Callaghan Guest Contributor

Sean Callaghan has over 20 years of experience in international development, including a decade coaching social entrepreneurs and facilitating leadership development. He has been a consultant for numerous organizations across Africa and the Middle East in the areas of strategic development, program design, strategic communications and conflict, and peace and reconciliation programs. He is married to Monica Callaghan and has three children. He planted and pastored a church in Johannesburg, South Africa, before moving to London six years ago.

Notes

Lecture 2: New Testament Considerations

1. Linda Belleville, "Teaching and Usurping Authority: 1 Timothy 2:11–15," in *Discovering Biblical Equality: Complementarity without Hierarchy*, ed. Rebecca M. Groothuis, Ronald W. Pierce, and Gordon D. Fee (Downers Grove, IL: Intervarsity, 2005), 205–23.

Lecture 3: A Historical Perspective

1. Aristotle, *Politica* 1.5.B4v, trans. Benjamin Jowett, vol. 10 in *The Works of Aristotle Translated into English Under the Editorship of W. D. Ross* (Oxford: Clarendon, 1921).
2. Plato, *Timaeus* 90e.
3. Irenaeus, Fragment 32, in *The Ante-Nicene Fathers*, ed. Philip Schaff (Grand Rapids: Eerdmans, 2001), 1:573.
4. Augustine, *On Marriage and Concupiscence* 1.10, trans. Robert Ernest Wallis, in *Nicene and Post-Nicene Fathers*, Series 1, ed. Philip Schaff [hereafter *NPNF*] (Grand Rapids: Eerdmans, 1886), 5:267.
5. John Chrysostom, "Homily IX," in *Homilies on 1 Timothy, NPNF* 13:436.
6. Jerome, "Preface to Commentary on Zephaniah" (PL 25:1337ff), quoted in *Great Inspirers*, by J. A. Zahm (New York: D. Appleton, 1917).
7. Frederick Edward Warren, *The Liturgy and Ritual of the Ante-Nicene Church* (New York: E. & J.B. Young, 1897), 312.
8. Aquinas, *Summa Theologiae* part I, question 93, article 4, trans. Fathers of the English Dominican Province (New York: Benziger Bros., 1947).
9. John Calvin, *Commentaries on the Epistles to Timothy, Titus and Philemon*, in *Calvin's Commentaries*, trans. William Pringle (Edinburgh: Calvin Translation Society, 1856), 37.
10. John Knox, "The First Blast of the Trumpet Against the Monstrous Regiment of Women 1558," in *The Political Writings of John Knox*, ed. Marvin A. Breslow (Cranbury, NY: Associated University Presses, 1985), 43.
11. Phoebe Palmer and Richard Wheatley, *The Life and Letters of Mrs. Phoebe Palmer* (New York: W.C. Palmer Publisher, 1876), 83.
12. A. J. Gordon, "The Ministry of Women," *Missionary Review of the*

World (1894): 910–21.

13. Katharine Bushnell, *Dr. Katharine C. Bushnell: A Brief Sketch of her Life and Work* (Hertford, UK: Rose and Sons Salisbury Square, 1930), 14.

14. Katharine Bushnell, *God's Word to Women: One Hundred Bible Studies on Woman's Place in the Church and Home* (Minneapolis, MN: Christians for Biblical Equality, 2003), 9, 10, 39–75.

15. Bushnell, *God's Word to Women*, 169.

16. Jessie Penn-Lewis, *The Climax of the Risen Life* (Bournemouth, UK: The Overcomer Book Room, originally published in 1909, 1946), 37.

Lecture 4: Opposing The Curse: Dismantling Patriarchy

1. Aristotle, *Politica* 1.5.B4v, trans. Benjamin Jowett, vol. 10 in *The Works of Aristotle*, ed. W. D. Ross (Oxford: Clarendon, 1921).

2. Manu IX:15–17. See the writings of Manu at http://www.hinduwebsite.com/sacredscripts/hinduism/dharma/manusmriti.asp, accessed June 2010.

3. Sahih al-Bukhari, Arabic-English translation, vol. 7, Hadith 113–14.

4. "Our Battle against Judah," German Propaganda Archive, Calvin College website, http://www.calvin.edu/academic/cas/gpa/rim3.htm.

5. Thornton Stringfellow, as quoted by Mark Noll, *The Civil War as a Theological Crisis* (Chapel Hill: UNC, 2006), 62.

6. Agenor de Gasparin, *The Uprising of a Great People*, trans. Mary Booth (New York: Scribners, 1862), 103–4.

7. John Chrysostom, "Homily IX," in *Homilies on 1 Timothy*, *NPNF* 13:436.

8. Augustine, *On Marriage and Concupiscence* 1.10, trans. Robert Ernest Wallis, *NPNF* 5:267.

9. John Knox, "The First Blast of the Trumpet against the Monstrous Regiment of Women 1558," in *The Political Writings of John Knox*, ed. Marvin A. Breslow (Cranbury, NY: Associate University Presses, 1985), 43.

10. John Calvin, *Commentaries on the Epistle to Timothy, Titus, and Philemon, in Calvin's Commentaries*, trans. William Pringle (Edinburgh: Calvin Translation Society, 1856), 37.

11. Mark Driscoll, Mars Hill Church, Seattle, WA. Quoted at http://www.dennyburk.com/mark-driscoll-on-women-in-ministry-2, accessed March 24, 2010.

12. Katharine Bushnell, *Dr. Katharine C. Bushnell: A Brief Sketch of her Life and Work* (Hertford, England: Rose and Sons Salisbury Square, 1930), 9.

13. Bushnell, *Dr. Katharine C. Bushnell*, 12.
14. Shuji G. Asai and David H. Olson, "Spouse Abuse and Marital System Based on ENRICH," University of Minnesota, https://www.prepare-enrich.com/pe_main_site_content/pdf/research/abuse.pdf. 3–4, 11; Nicholas D. Kristoff and Sheryl WuDunn, *Half the Sky: Turning Oppression into Opportunity for Women Worldwide* (New York: Vintage, 2009) xiv–xv; "Gendercide," *The Economist*, March 2010, http://www.economist.com/node/15606229.
15. For each country cited, the author published his or her accounts in: "A Consistent Witness: Christian Leaders Consider Religious Patriarchy and Social Justice," *Ideas Have Consequences*, 19–20, available from CBE at http://www.cbeinternational.org/sites/default/files/Ideas-Have-Consequences-reprint-web.pdf.
16. *Mahabharata*, Anusasana Parva, Section XXXVIII, trans. Sri Kisari Mohan Ganguli. The same text appears also in Sri Shiva Mahapurana Uma Samhita Ch 24.
17. Goswami Tulsidas. *Śrī Rāmacaritamānasa*, canto 5 "Sundar Kand." Some versions say "instruction" instead of "beating." See *Śrī Rāmacaritamānasa* (Gorakhpur, India: Gita, 2004), 820, http://www.gitapress.org/books/1318/1318_Sri%20Ramchritmanas_Roman.pdf, accessed June 16, 2015.
18. *Mahabhatara*, Anusasana Parva, Section CXLVI, trans. Sri Kisari Mohan Ganguli.
19. Robinson, Lance. "A Matter of Justice: My Journey Toward Gender Equality." *Arise* E-Newsletter, Christians for Biblical Equality, October 6, 2011. Available at https://www.cbeinternational.org/resource/article/mutuality-blog-magazine/matter-justice-my-journey-toward-gender-equality.

Lecture 5: Working Cross-Culturally

1. "The 6-D model of national culture," Geert Hofstede Centre, https://geerthofstede.com/culture-geert-hofstede-gert-jan-hofstede/6d-model-of-national-culture/

Additional Resources

1. Free articles and journals from CBE International, available at www.cbeinternational.org.

2. Bainton, Roland. *Women of the Reformation*. Beacon Press, 1971.

3. Brauch, Manfred. *Abusing Scripture: The Consequences of Misreading the Bible*. Carol Stream, IL: Intervarsity, 2009.

4. Bushnell, Katharine. *God's Word to Women: One Hundred Bible Studies on Woman's Place in the Church and Home*. Minneapolis: Christians for Biblical Equality, 2003.

5. Chilcote, Paul. *Early Methodist Spirituality: Selected Women's Writings*. Nashville: Kingswood, 2007.

6. Drummond, Lewis and Betty. *Women of Awakenings: A Historic Contribution of Women to Revival Movements*. Grand Rapids: Kregel, 1997.

7. Kavanagh, Julia. *Women of Christianity*. Eugene, OR: Wipf & Stock, 2006.

8. Osiek, Carolyn and Margaret MacDonald. *A Woman's Place*. Minneapolis: Fortress, 2006.

9. Taylor, Marion Ann and Agnes Choi, editors, *Handbook of Women Biblical Interpreters: A Historical and Biographical Guide*. Grand Rapids: Baker, 2012.

Printed in the USA
CPSIA information can be obtained
at www.ICGtesting.com
LVHW052347010224
770657LV00048B/1059

9 781939 971944